FLORA IN FOCUS

JAPANESE GARDENS

TIGER BOOKS INTERNATIONAL
LONDON

This edition published in 1996 by
Tiger Books International PLC, Twickenham

Photographs:
PPWW Plant Pictures World Wide, Daan Smit
Text:
Carla Teune
Translation:
Ildikó Nemes
Concept and editing:
Boris van Dobbenburgh
Design:
Meijster Design
Color Separation:
Unifoto PTY LTD, Cape Town
Production:
Agora United Graphic Services, 's-Graveland
Printing and binding:
Egedsa, Sabadell, Spain

ISBN 1-85501-826-8

INTRODUCTION

The long chain of islands that together forms Japan, includes a variety of temperature zones. In the north the prevailing climate produces very cold winters with a heavy snowfall every year. The summers are warm with plenty of rain for good plant growth. In contrast to Hokkaido, the largest northern island (45 degrees north latitude), the largest southern island, Kyushu (30 degrees north latitude) has a subtropical climate, whilst between these two extremities all possible variations exist. It is, therefore, not surprising because of these climactic variations to find that Japan is a land extraordinarily suited for rich flora. Bearing in mind that there are mountain regions with their own very specific plant life as well as the different coastal regions (the flora from the mild coastal regions bordering the Pacific is completely different from the flora on the coasts bordering the Sea of Japan and the East China Sea), it is clear that there are many opportunities for optimal growth of very diverse and interesting plant species.

It is perhaps astonishing to learn that during the early period of horticulture in Japan a large number of plants were imported from China and found a home in Japan. Was the immense body of plant material insufficient for the Japanese, or was it a case of 'the grass is greener on the other side', like in Europe many centuries later? Just as it was popular among the upper class during the late Renaissance to speak French, it was also fashionable in Japan during the first years of the Heian period (especially in the newly founded capital Heiankyo with its important family the Fujiwara's, who played second fiddle only to the emperor's family) to copy cultural influences from China.

Many of the existing gardens in Japan date back to a period that was very important for the Japanese culture; a time when the old Shinto religion (an indigenous religion marked by the worship of nature spirits) was almost surpassed by the new religion that came from China: Buddhism.

The exact date that Buddhism was firmly established in Japan is not known. The most common estimate is the middle of the 6th century A.D. It is known that Buddhism spread like wildfire over the islands and had a strong influence on life in Japan.

It shouldn't be surprising to the reader that there are so many temple gardens included in this book. Shintoistic temple gardens are also included, very often with an especially old or extremely imposing tree as the centerpiece, clearly recognizable as divine by the straw cord (shimenawa) hung around it. The shimenawa indicates the tree's sanctity and at the same time repels angry spirits.

The Ise-jingu Shrine from the 3rd century is one of the most visited and admired Shinto sanctuaries in Japan. The 1000 year old Gingko tree in the city of Sendai is also included in this book and is a good example of a Shinto deity worshipped to this day. Some of the most famous Buddhist temple gardens are those of the large Buddhist temple complex from Eihei-ji, the Kongo-bu-ji in Koyason and the most famous of all Zen Buddhist temples: Ryoan-ji in Kyoto.

In later centuries there was a harmonious integration of Shinto and Buddhist influences and that is still apparent in many gardens. For example, water basins that come from Shintoism are quite frequently used in Zen Buddhist temple gardens. These basins are used for the ritual cleansing of the mouth and hands before people enter the temple. One of these water basins can be found in the most correct and strict example of a Zen garden in the Ryoan-ji garden in Kyoto.

This gives the impression that Japanese gardens are attached strictly to temples, there are however important existing gardens that were planted next to palaces - even from the Heian period.

Perfect imitations of nature are also characteristic of Japanese gardening. The large pond that reflects the image of the Golden Pavilion, (Kinkaku-ji in Kyoto) looks like it was created by nature, however it was expressly excavated by Shogun Yoshimitsu in order to create a breathtaking effect. Raked, silver-gray gravel often symbolizes the sea (Ryoan-ji, Kyoto) or moonbeams (Silver Pavilion, Kyoto) and even the holy mountain Fuji-san can be found in miniature in gardens.

Garden ornaments are always placed because of their beauty, but they also always have a symbolic meaning. Stepping stones in a pond are placed especially so that someone taking a walk can reach the other side with dry feet, but they also symbolize our path in the journey of life. Stone or bronze lanterns, that are lit only few times each year, are well-planned accents in the garden's design and at the same time they symbolize the light shining on the path of life.

Contrasts are also an unmistakable part of Japanese gardens. Round, pruned rhododendron bushes are placed for their green, round form and between them a single, strategically placed bush will be planted that blooms with an exuberant, bright pink contrast in the late fall.

A path in a garden will never bring a pedestrian straight through from one place to the other, but wanders zigzag and when a path cuts through a section of a garden as if drawn by a ruler, people can be certain that the stones used as pavement have been placed in surprising patterns or that a special paving material was used. There are too many contrasts and surprises in a Japanese garden to list them all in this small space. That should certainly never hinder a visitor, in contrast the visitor will look forward with expectations to the next garden and the interesting images it has to offer.

Gardens with a special plant theme, such as moss gardens, are also very special and characteristic of Japan. Mosses are known to be very difficult to cultivate; it is actually only the Japanese who have accepted the challenge, encouraged by the favorable damp climate where many moss species grow exceptionally well.

It is also almost impossible to think of a country where the population devotes itself so much to looking at flowers: the great interest in the profusion of blossom carried by the Oriental Cherry in the spring is one of the best examples.

JISHO-JI, SILVER PAVILION, KYOTO

The most famous gardens in Japan belong to the Silver Pavilion (Ginkaku-ji). The pavilion was built in 1479 as the country house for Shogun Yoshimasa. This splendid building is simpler and more austere in shape than the Gold Pavilion (Kinko-ku-ji) that is also in Kyoto. Although it has the name 'Silver' Pavilion, it was never finished with silver. The garden, credited to So-ami, consists of two contrasting sections; a classical garden with ponds and a dry natural landscape garden. The latter, with its silver sand, gravel and stones symbolizing the sea and the mountains, breaths with the spirit of Zen Buddhism.

JISHO-JI, SILVER PAVILION, KYOTO

Sand hill, built from meticulously raked gravel interspersed with bands of silver sand. This symbolizes the slanting moonbeams. This garden structure is very typical of a Zen Buddhist garden in the dry style (karesansui.) The contrast with the natural landscape garden in which topiary shrubs catch the eye, can hardly be greater. But it is exactly these contrasts that the unsuspecting foreign visitor frequently finds in Japanese horticulture.

NANZEN-JI TEMPLE, KYOTO

Rock garden with silver colored gravel raked to form waves designed in the dry style (karesansui.) The garden is enclosed by a wall that is covered by gray earthenware roofing tile, characteristic of many Japanese gardens. The low, round bumps alongside the gravel waves are neatly clipped bushes and in the left hand corner a lovely pine (*Pinus*) has been carefully clipped to shape. The upkeep of this garden is very labor intensive: there is never a fallen leaf on the gravel and as soon as young shoots begin to grow, the shrub is carefully clipped back into shape.

The temple was originally built as a villa for Emperor Kameyama. After his death in 1291, the building was consecrated as a Zen temple.

KONGOBU-JI, KOYASAN
This rock garden, belonging to the main temple (Kondo or Hondo) of 'the Vatican' of the Sjingon sect, lies at an altitude of 860 meters. The expansive temple complex has more than 120 buildings including the famous Temple of 10,000 lanterns. A Buddhist school and a museum with exceptionally beautiful treasures of religious art can also be found here. The garden is laid out in the dry style and reminds one of a rocky coastal landscape dotted with Japanese maples (*Acer japonicum*) and their lovely fall colors that form a wonderful contrast with the two dark conifers in the background. In the meticulously raked gravel sea are a few stones that symbolize islands.

KIYOMIZUDERA TEMPLE, KYOTO

Before the worshippers enter a Shinto temple, they must first visit the symbolic cleansing place. Beautiful rock water basins with fresh, clear water flowing into them have been placed by the entrance for that purpose. The worshippers scoop up water in a ladle and cleanse their hands and mouth, only after completing this ritual are they permitted to enter the temple to fulfill their religious obligations. The water spouts are often brilliant masterpieces of bronze casting, such as the scaled, winged dragon in the photo.

JISHO-JI SILVER PAVILION, KYOTO

The landscape design of this famous and frequently visited garden is beautifully revealed by the winding path that meanders through a moss arrangement and along the stone edge of a clear pond. This imitation of nature is accentuated by the crooked pine that leans towards another of its kind forming a natural gateway. The temple seems to be tucked away in nature, even though that nature was created by human hands.

KOISHIKAWA KORAKUEN GARDEN, OKAYAMA NEAR TOKYO

This famous garden was designed in the landscape style by Ikeda Tsunamase around 1700. The shrubs are meticulously pruned into lovely round forms and symbolize stones in a landscape. Although most of the plants are pruned so closely that the buds cannot develop and the ball-form shrubs remain green through out the whole year, there are a few strategically planted shrubs (in the photo: a hybrid of the *Rhododendron obtusum*, a native Japanese Rhododendron species) that bloom in the spring. In this manner, contrasts are continually created, sometimes in the way a plant grows and sometimes, as in this garden, with color.

KYU-FURUKAWA GARDEN, TOKYO

The large, venerable old shrubs have been pruned into a round shape which prevent them flowering. These imitate a rocky landscape with unpruned trees, that have been left to grow, forming a natural background.

RHODODENDRON OBTUSUM HYBRIDS, KORAKAMI

A group of perfectly clipped *Rhododendron obtusum* hybrids that are pruned in such a way that they imitate a rocky landscape with their big green round shape for nearly the entire year. The art of pruning (Korakomi) these Rhododendrons to shape is to leave just enough on the shrub that they can indeed bloom in the spring and can delight the eye of the visitor with their brilliant colors. A contrast is also created with the dark leaves of the trees to the right in the background.

KATSURA IMPERIAL VILLA, KYOTO

In Japanese horticulture, a garden is often surrounded by a wall, a fence, a hedge, or any combination of these. The construction of high or low bamboo garden fences has developed into an art in itself. In order to make a beautiful fence, bamboo stalks of the same length and the same thickness are carefully selected. Bamboo with a spotted or striped pattern is sometines chosen. No nails are used in the making of such a splendid fence. Only rope is used (the use of natural materials is preferred) and this is worked into the fence in many different ways. As the centuries have passed there have been large books written over the use of rope and how to harmonise it with the bamboo stalks. Knots and rope bindings are extensively described and drawn.

HEIAN-JINGU SHRINE, KYOTO
The Heian Shrine is famous throughout Japan for its Oriental cherry (Sakura) blossom in April. Bamboo racks are placed under the branches in order to support their heavy cargo of blossoms and give them the best opportunity to develop. Thousands of visitors come yearly to enjoy the blooming of these cherry blossoms.

RYOAN-JI TEMPLE, KYOTO
A quiet corner inside the park at Ryoan-ji Temple. A sturdy bamboo fence separates the low, neatly clipped hedge from the strolling visitors and emphasizes the large, linked spherical shapes of the shrubs.

RYOGEN-IN TEMPLE, KYOTO
The garden by the Ryogen-in Temple is strongly influenced by Zen Buddhism. It is one of the most famous Japanese moss gardens, where numerous moss species, that are difficult to grow, are planted. The maintenance of such moss gardens is a meticulous task: every small weed must be removed from the moss carpet as early as possible in order to minimize possible damage to the delicate mosses. A zigzag path flanked by a few round green shrubs comes as a surprise. In a Zen garden paths are not only made for walking on, they also symbolize the path of life made by man, a path that also seldom runs true, regardless of how much we may desire a straight path through life.

PAVING IN A JAPANESE GARDEN

Materials are used in many ways for ornamental paving in Japanese gardens. Small, square basalt stones are arranged here in attractive circles, in what seems to be a normal lawn, however, instead of grass the compactly growing *Ophiopgen japonicus* variety is used. This is a small plant that belongs to the Lily family and is used in many Japanese gardens.

KOISHIKAWA KORAKUEN GARDEN, TOKYO

A path of stepping stones meanders through a dark pond like rounded islands. Stepping stones (tobiishi) with diverse forms and created from different materials are often used. They are not only used as a path to walk on, but also have a symbolic meaning: with every stone a person is a step closer to the goal. Such stepping stones are never placed in a straight line; that provides no surprises.

GARDEN OF THE IMPERIAL PALACE, TOKYO

In Japanese garden architecture, wherever there is water there is almost always a bridge or stepping stones in order to cross the water. This arched bridge, built in a lovely wet garden laid out in landscape style, is a true garden ornament. The uprights of the bridge railing have bronze decorations in the form of ancient ornaments. Such decorations are often used not only on the bridges but also on temple galleries. As is so often the case, these bridges have a double use, practical and symbolic.

KYU-FURUKAWA GARDEN, TOKYO

Stone or bronze lanterns (Toro) are one of the most commonly used garden ornaments and are always built from five parts. The toro is always placed in an exceptionally lovely place in the garden so that they are easily seen and can be appreciated. The lanterns are usually precision-carved from natural stone and only on rare occasions will you see a lantern that looks like it was made of coarse natural stones stacked carelessly upon each other. Nothing could be further from the truth. Although the lanterns form a contrast to their surroundings, they actually bring harmony in subtle ways. They not only serve as garden ornaments, but are also lit twice a year. The lanterns are lit on February 3 during the exorcism of the dark wind spirits and again on August 15 during Bon, the Buddhist feast for the dead.

CHERRY IN BLOOM
No other language in the world has a special word for 'looking at flowers.' In Japanese the word: Hanami (Hana=flower) has been around for centuries. Around mid-April, when the blossoms of the Oriental Cherry or Sakura unfurl in their full glory, Japanese families or large groups of school children journey specially to temple complexes to gaze at the blossoms of the Sakura and enjoy a picnic lunch. The cherry blossoms are at their most beautiful just before they fall, and the petals fluttering to the ground on a soft breeze or a delicate carpet of fallen blossom also draw gasps of wonder. The best moment for blossom depends on many factors, and because of this, the press has a 'flower report' for the Sakura in many cities. The flower report is called 'Sakura-dayori'.

ROKKAKU-DO TEMPLE, TOKYO
A greater contrast than can be seen in this photo hardly seems possible: the severe vertical columns of the temple and in front of them an Oriental Cherry (Sakura) laden with flowers. Tucked away between the

trees is a lovely bronze statue of Buddha. This *Prunus serrulatea* hybrid reaches the height of her glory in early spring when it is covered with double flowers.

JUNIPERUS CHINENSIS 'KAIZUKA'

Dark green conifers do not need to be dull or sober, as proven by this lovely clipped hybrid of the Chinese Juniper. Nevertheless it is very important that the trees are expertly cultivated from a young age. This very large specimen is in the Botanical Garden of Kanogawa and has reached a ripe old age through good care.

SHINYUKU GYOEN NATIONAL GARDEN, TOKYO

In the background is a respectable pine tree, pruned as a gigantic bonsai and in the foreground are a few shrubs clipped into round shapes to suggest that the pine is growing in a natural landscape with large boulders.

Juniperus chinensis 'Kaizuka' is perfectly suited for trimming into beautiful round forms. The illusion is created of an old wall overgrown with moss and a few large boulders loosely stacked on top. This exceptionally and skillfully nurtured imitation wall is a good example of what the art of topiary can create. The hedge also serves as a dense impenetrable barrier between pathways. This example of a gardener's expertise can be found in the Botanical Garden of Kanogawa. Through the centuries, the Japanese have proven very inventive in their use of a large assortment of plants for making smooth hedges and constructions clipped in to ball shapes. Evergreens such as conifers, a few species of small-leafed holly (*Ilex*), (*Euonymus*) and shrub honey suckle (*Lonicera Pileata*) are very popular, but deciduous trees and plants are also readily used, especially if lovely colored berries appear on the shrub in the autumn, or the leaves turn to many colors in the fall, from red, to orange to gold.

KINKAJU-JI, KYOTO
This lovely example of the art of Bonsai can be found next to one of the annexes of the Golden Pavilion in Kyoto. This is a pine species (*Pinus species*) raised in the form of a ship, such as those that sailed around Japan in earlier centuries. To help this very old specimen to keep its form, the tree is supported by a sturdy construction of bamboo racks.

RIKUGIEN GARDEN, TOKYO
The elegant branches of a respectable old pine bending over the water look very natural, however, they have actually been carefully pruned in the form of clouds. To keep the old, very heavy branches from breaking, they are supported by sturdy poles. Such large old specimens are extremely valuable even though their value is less in terms of money than of beauty.

KOISHIKAWA KORAKUEN GARDEN, TOKYO

The extremely contorted trunk of an old pine (*Pinus species*) is protected against weather by straw. The tree has an almost reptilian appearance, caused by the rough dark-colored rope used to bind the straw around the trunk. This protection is apparently necessary because the tree (after a fire or some other disaster) lost part of its bark. The straw wrap acts as a second skin and could help keep this lovely conifer alive for years and keep the tree's function as eyecatcher in this garden. This tree was planted by Ikeda Tsunamase when this famous landscape garden was first laid out in about 1700.

UKIMIDO TEMPLE, BIWA LAKE NEAR KYOTO

The Biwa lake is a short distance from Kyoto (15 km) and is easy to reach by train, car or bus. A visit to the many temples surrounding this lake is a must, not least because of the peaceful atmosphere created by the lake and the lovely trees in the gardens and parks belonging to the many temples. The Ukimido Temple (floating temple) lies on the left bank of the lake and belongs to the vast temple complex of Isjiyamadera. The atmosphere invites the visitor to meditate and contemplate. The small building that stands in the water on wooden beams is built entirely from wood without using a single nail. The open construction of the wooden piles supporting the building and the typical Japanese curve of the eaves of the roof gives the building the appearance of a crane hovering over the water.

KOISHIKAWA KARAKUEN GARDEN, TOKYO

In this elegant corner of a Shinto garden, a simple, round water basin overgrown with a lovely brown moss, catches the eye. The neatly woven bamboo screen, made from thin stalks arranged in a diagonal pattern forms a beautiful background for a group of *Apidistras*, a single fern and a tender, young tree.

RAKKAKU-DO TEMPLE, TOKYO

In a small hexagon of carefully assembled smooth round pebbles a hexagonal water basin lies practically hidden under the overhanging branches of a Mahonia bush. Pieces of paper bearing blessings adorn the Mahonia bush. The strips of paper can be acquired by shaking a bamboo cylinder so that one of the good luck sticks fall out. The number on the stick shaken out of the bamboo cylinder indicates the number on the piece of paper and the pilgrim carefully ties his paper to a shrub on the temple grounds. Birds are also used to choose one lucky stick from a collection. The blessing should bring the pilgrim luck. Sometimes there are more white strips of paper on a bush than leaves!

RYOAN-JI TEMPLE, KYOTO

Behind the main temple (Hondo) of the famous rock garden Ryoan-ji in Kyoto is a lovely, round stone water basin (tsukubai) for the ritual cleansing. It is very reminiscent of an ancient copper Chinese coin with a hole. These coins are placed on a string and a full string with copper coins had a certain value. To think of money in a Zen temple is distasteful, even though it is necessary to pay an entrance fee and souvenirs are for sale. The four characters on the edge of the basin mean 'only I know if I am satisfied' which is a typical expression of the true humbleness in Zen Buddhism that invites one to meditate.

KATSURA RIKYU IMPERIAL VILLA, KYOTO

The Katsura Imperial Villa continues in our time to serve as an example of modern architecture. The neat simplicity appeals to present-day architects and the villa, which was build on the west bank of the Katsura river between 1620 - 1624 for Prince Toshihito, is a frequent source of inspiration. The park is one of the loveliest in Japan and every detail of the buildings, the garden with a charming pond, tea houses, lanterns, trees, shrubs, islands and stones are all carefully looked after.

RYOAN-JI TEMPLE, KYOTO

Here we see a barrel-shaped bridge, with, in the background, an orange-red torii or the holy gateway to a Shinto temple. Even though the Ryoan-ji Temple is a Zen-Buddhist sanctuary, the placing of the Shinto torii clearly indicates the mix of Shintoism and Buddhism.

A torii is a high archway with a symbolic meaning. It is often made from painted wood, but sometimes it is carved from gray stone. When the pilgrims pass under the archway, they leave the night behind them and enter into the day. In this way people go through a spiritual re-birth on their way to the Shinto Shrine. If we realize that Shinto roughly means 'the way of the kami (god)' then the torii fits precisely in this view. A torii can sometimes be found close to the entrance of a Shinto sanctuary, but toriis can also be found on a road quite a distance away or in a densely built-up street in the city. This suggests that the original temple grounds were considerably larger than is the case today.

KONCHI-IN, NANZEN-JI, KYOTO

A charming round pond where young, red colored water lily leaves provide a surprising contrast to the neatly clipped green shrubs and the mirror-like clear pond water. Our gaze is irrepressibly drawn to the bridge of two stone monoliths that cut off the pond from our viewing angle, but which at the same time offers a crossing for pedestrians. The torii opens the path over the bridge. The elegant garden was originally planted in the 17th century by the famous garden designer Kobori Enshu who was one of the most important masters of the tea ceremony in his time.

JUNIPERIS CHINENSIS

Two lovely old bonsai trees, where attention is drawn not only to the conifers (above: *Juniperus chinensis*, below, *Picea glehnii*), but also to the receptacle in which they are planted. Such receptacles form a very important part of the art of bonsai, they must form a harmonious whole with the bonsai or intentionally deliver a surprising contrast. Such pots or trays can be made from pottery, porcelain, wood or metal. Often the larger specimens are unique and extremely expensive. Bonsai is a centuries old, highly specialized manner of caring for trees and shrubs. The roots are wrapped in thin iron wire; soil, water and fertilizer are sparingly provided, and with careful pruning starting from a very young age and much patience lovely specimens are obtained that can live for decades, even for centuries becoming priceless. It is a challenge and an art to care for a tree in this way, so that they don't grow to their true size, but stay miniature. Nevertheless they do flower and bear fruit, which is extremely spectacular, given how large these trees can be in their natural state.

ZELKOVA SERRATEA - BONSAI

The *Zelkova serratea* (Keyaki), a native Japanese tree that can grow as tall as the White Elm can develop, with much care, into a bonsai. It is small, even though a thick trunk is formed. The lovely golden orange fall colors of the leaves makes this tree very inviting to develop as a bonsai. Small groups of very young Zelkova seedlings are also often used in miniature landscapes. The Zelkova is a very strong tree and for that reason it is perfectly suited as a street or avenue tree; they are often planted in cities with high levels of air pollution, such as Tokyo and Kyoto.

FUTARA SAN JINJA SHRINE, NIKKO

A number of small temples lie in a stately cedar forest, where, because it is peaceful and quiet, it is very pleasant to linger a little and take a look around. There are delightful corners to be found: a pond that is surrounded by large, round stones, a beautiful natural stone lantern and a simple round water basin where water splashes in from a man-made stream. The shrine built by Shodo Shonin in the early part of the 17th century is consecrated to three gods of prosperity: the mountain, Nantai, the wife of this mountain, Nyotai and their mountain child, Taro.

FUTARA SAN JINJA SHRINE, NIKKO

Two worthy examples of the native Japanese conifer *Cryptomeria japonica* (Sugi). These trees are gods (kami) of the Shinto religion and in order to make their holiness visible, straw cords(shimenawa) are wrapped around the tree with gokei hanging from the cord. Gokei are zigzag folded or trimmed paper strips that symbolize the many hands of the Kami. Such straw cords also act as protection from angry spirits. In Hakone lies a lake which is more than 2 kilometers long as well as an avenue of Sugi that are more than 350 years old and it is very impressive to walk along such an old Cryptomeria avenue.

TOSHOGU SHRINE, NIKKO

The exuberantly and colorfully decorated shrine was built between 1634 - 1636 by Iemitsu, the grandson of the famous Shogun Ieyasu, to honor his famous grandfather. Ieyasu's bronze tomb can be visited by climbing a stairway with 200 steps. In the buildings two Japanese styles can be found: the Momoyama style and the Edo style, but the decorations are typical Ming Chinese; that is apparent in the golden roofs, where Chinese figures can be seen. The blue and gold of the wooden artifacts are also typical Chinese.

TOSHOGO SHRINE, NIKKO

The carved wooden panel on the stable of the holy horses, is attributed to the famous Japanese wood carver Hidari Jingoro. It is the famous three monkeys sitting in the stylized pine tree expressing the famous image 'hear no evil, say no evil, see no evil'. The extensive temple complex with a large number of magnificent buildings is worth an extended visit in every respect, even though it is a very busy tourist attraction.

TSUROGAODA HACHIMANGU SHRINE, KAMAKURA

Barrels of sake as a gift for the temple. It is not only the wealth of the temple that is demonstrated by the large number of barrels, but it also allows the religious donors of these sake barrels to show how well-off they are.

Sake or rice wine is the national liquor of Japan, distilled from rice by a complicated process. There are many different qualities of sake and it should be warmed in small porcelain jugs. Sake is usually drunk from small porcelain bowls, but sometimes small square cedarwood boxes (ichi-go) are used. The people in Japan say that the cedarwood adds something of itself to the aroma and taste of the sake.

TOSHOGU SHRINE, NIKKO
The barrels of sake that are intended as a gift to a temple are often beautifully decorated with large Japanese script. They are written with a writing pencil made from a brush (fude) that is dipped in a black ink (sumi.) Japanese and Chinese ink is supplied as ink sticks that are mixed with water to create ink. An ink pot can be a very beautiful handmade antique, the small water pot is also often expensive porcelain. Even the more expensive versions of ink stones have beautiful golden script. Writing or calligraphy (shodo) is also an old, highly respected art.

TOSHOGU SHRINE, NIKKO
Sake barrels are not always adorned with large, bold script, they are also often decorated with in-season flowers. Given that white Chrysanthemum (kiku) have been painted on this barrel, this drink will most probably be given to the Toshogu Shrine in the fall.

RINNO-JI TEMPLE, NIKKO

A row of beautiful bronze lanterns (toro) stand near one of the elegant and wonderfully decorated temple buildings of the Rinno-ji Temple complex. The main building, the Sanbutsu-do was built in 848 by the Buddhist priest Jihaku Daishi. In this building are three wooden statues of Buddha, each of them seated on a Sacred Lotus flower. The statue on the right, the Senju, is the Kannon with 1,000 hands. When carefully counted, it appears that the statue is in possession of 'only' 40 hands, each hand symbolizing 25 wishes. The statue on the left is Bato Kannon, the Buddha that concerns himself with the animal kingdom. This diety is recognized by the horse head. The statue in the middle is Amida-Nyorai.

In this temple hall there is also a bronze pillar erected in 1643 that is 15 meters high and 3 meters in diameter, the Sorinto, that symbolizes world peace and contains 1,000 holy sutras. Holy sutras are the written doctrines of Buddha, the Lotus Sutra is considered in Japan as the only true doctrine.

TOSHOGU SHRINE, NIKKO

This row of beautiful old stone lanterns stands in front of one of the buildings of the imposing Toshogu complex, the final resting place of the remains of Shogun Tokugawa Iyeasu. Whilst the lanterns appear very uniform at first glance, a closer look shows that no two are the same, typical of the true crafts of artists.

RINNO-JI TEMPLE, NIKKO
On a carpet of green moss stands a small army of old stone lanterns as guards next to a small temple. Even though stone lanterns (ishidori), just like all the other lanterns in Japan, are supposed to be lit twice a year, it seems hardly possible with this group because of the luxurious growth of ferns. There are two important days in Japan when all the lanterns are lit: on February 3 during the ceremony to exorcise the dark wind spirits and on August 15 during Bon, the feast for the dead for Buddhism. Just like many ornaments in Japanese gardens, the lanterns are not only meant to be lit, they also symbolize the points of light along the pathway of life.

Not only do the luxuriant ferns create an unusual effect on these lanterns, but the mosses and lichens make the lanterns more interesting and attractive in the eyes of the Japanese (and not only in their eyes).

TOSHOGU SHRINE, NIKKO

This small group of fine, old stone temple lanterns in the grounds of the rich and important Toshogu complex harmonizes wonderfully with the small building and its decoratively curved roof. The temple complex lies in a wooded area containing centuries old conifers and was built between 1634 - 1636 by Iemitsu, the grandson of the great Shogun Iyeasu. Ieyasu was one of the three Shoguns who, at the end of the 16th century when Japan was divided and at war, was able to forge a strong empire.

KINKAKU-JI TEMPLE, KYOTO
The renowned Golden Temple is reflected in the large pond. The building was constructed by Shogun Ashikago Yoshim in 1397 as a place in which to spend the last years of his life. Together with groups of friends he held meetings (tsukumi) where they gazed at the moon for hours and wrote poems about the moon. After his death, it became a Zen Buddhist temple of the Rinzai sect.

The building burnt to the ground in 1950, after being set on fire by a young monk. It was rebuilt in 1955. The famous Japanese writer, Mishimi Yukio wrote about this drama in his famous book 'The Golden Temple'. After the gold leaf was found to be flaking off (in the early 80's), the building was completely restored. At the same time, the ground floor was also finished with gold leaf, a true labor of love, given that every piece of gold leaf had to be fixed to the wooden background by hand. The roofing is made of small wooden planks laid overlapping so that the beautiful curved eaves could be shaped. The golden phoenix (ho-o), that crowns the roof is a true symbol of the burning of the temple and its resurrection on its own ashes. The pretentious building, that is understandable called, 'the high point of untouchable beauty' stands in a lovely park. The garden is an example of Muromachi landscape architecture. Shogun Yoshimitsu also had the magnificent pond dug in which the building is reflected. Although this temple is visited by bus loads of tourists daily, a tranquil atmosphere still exists and the visitors politely give each other plenty of room and opportunity to take exactly the same photos.

IMAKUMANO SHRINE, KYOTO
A beautiful combination of various roof forms at this Shinto temple: a high pointed roof, that is slightly curved with, in front of it, a pretty arched roof above the entrance. The straw cord (shimenawa) indicates that this is a sanctuary. The cord offers protections against angry spirits. The folded or trimmed zig-zag strips of white paper (gokei) symbolize the many hands of the kami or deity. The lovely tall tree behind the temple is a Camphor tree (*Cinnamomum camphora*) planted in 1127 and is an impressive specimen. The symbolic significance of the holy *Ficus* in Indiase Buddhism is, in Japan, given to the Camphor tree.

ACER PALMATUM
It is almost impossible to think of a tree with more brilliant fall colors than the Japanese Maple (*Acer palmatum*.) This tree is not only often planted in temple complexes, it is also a tremendously popular tree for bonsai culture and for private gardens. The combination of the red-brown Acer with the orange painted fence is daring but well-balanced and harmonious.

NELUMBO IOTUS
The Sacred Lotus has not only been planted in temple ponds, but it has also been a favorite garden plant in Japan for centuries. It is a plant full of contrasts: the soft green round leaves with their thin stems rise from the stinking mud in the spring to stand high above the water. In the summer, lovely, mostly delicate pink colored large flowers bloom. The leaves and flowers wither in the fall, leaving the beautiful seed pods to stand above the water for a long time. The Sacred Lotus is not only a flower that is admired in the Buddhist religion, but also a plant that produces food. The roots are eaten and also the seeds, after they are roasted in order to burn off poisonous substances. For centuries, Japanese gardeners have been cross-breeding these plants and there are now specimens that have pure white flowers, some specimens with double flowers and there is even a miniature form that can be raised in gardens or in pretty porcelain pots.

ROUND PRUNED PLANTS AND TREES

A more beautiful picture of various shrubs pruned in round forms could hardly be find. The low balls, almost carelessly planted between beautiful large stones, are pruned Rhododendrons. The large tree that is to the left of the stone with the inscription is a pine (*Pinus*) and the tree on the right is a *Cryptomeria japonica* (Sugi.) Perhaps such pruning goes too far for our western tastes, but in Japanese eyes these master works of horticulture are accorded the utmost respect.

SHIRAKAWA-GO, NEAR SOGIMACHI

The open air museum of Shirakawa-go consists of a collection of houses built in the Gassho-zukuri architectural style. There are a number of such houses assembled from the surrounding area; in a few houses demonstrations are given of old trades, such as working with wood or straw, the manufacturing of pottery in the traditional manner and the making of paintings with black ink. These articles can also be purchased. In the photo is a ritual wash basin, made from roughly finished stone, alongside which pink and white flowering Begonias, an imported plant, are planted annually.

DAIHONZEN EIHEI-JI TEMPLE, YOSHIDA-GUN

The Zen temple established by Dogen in 1244 currently consists of 70 buildings and has developed through the centuries into one of the most important temples of the Soro sect. The vast complex lies in an old cypress forest (Hinoki or *Chamaecyparis obtusa*, a native Japanese conifer) with the oldest trees dating back to the 13th century. They symbolize the rock-solid hold Zen-Buddhism has developed in Japan. The Eihi-ji Temple provides guests, including foreigners, with the chance to follow Zen training. Candidates must apply by writing well in advance, because students are expected to remain in the temple complex during their training.

TETSUGAKU-NO MICHI, KYOTO

For centuries the Philosophy Path in Kyoto has been a short walk (about 30 minutes) in a natural area. The walk begins at the Eikan-do Temple and ends at the Ginkaku-ji Pavilion. In the middle of the city it possible to walk along deep in thought, or simply enjoying the beautiful plants along a stream. It appears that nature has been given a free hand, but nothing could be further from the truth: the plants were chosen with great care and the Philosophy Path is maintained with the most painstaking care. In the spring, when the cherry trees bloom, the observer can enjoy not only the blossoming trees, but also the light filtering through the blossoms. When a light breeze sends the soft pink petals fluttering down like light snow, with a few of the petals coming to rest on the water, the Japanese consider this to be one of the sublime moments.

SALIX BABYLONICA

This weeping willow (*Salix Babylonica*) carried, in earlier times, the more fitting Latin name, *Salix pendula* (hanging willow.) The specimen shown was planted near the Rokkaku-do Temple in 906 and the tree is now 1090 years old, which is an extraordinary age for a willow. In Japan this willow is called Rokkaku, and it is reasonable to suppose that the temple was named after the tree. Contrasts are sought for here in this setting, the hanging, soft green branches of the willow creating a surprising effect alongside the large, horizontally trained bonsai pine.

AMANO HASHIDATE, MIYAZU CITY

True 'works of art' in the clipped and forced shapes of the cedar trees (*Cedrus deodara*, originated from the Himalaya area.) Cedars are not easy to cultivate into such artistic forms, the process has to be started when the saplings are still very young and supple.

TSUROGAOKA HACHIMANGU SHRINE, KAMAKURA

Tree peonies (*Paeonia suffruticosa*) are much loved in Japan and China and have been raised there for a long time. Originally these tree peonies with woody branches (not to be confused with the perennial garden peony) come from China. They are, like many other Chinese plants, extremely popular in Japan. The tree peony (*Botan*) is often planted in Japanese gardens, usually as a single specimen, because of its elegant and yet sturdy growth, but especially because of its lovely flowers in attractively colored soft tints.

HASEDERA TEMPLE, KAMAKURA

Kamakura, once the capital of the Japanese Empire (1192-1333), has a large number of temple complexes. The famous giant Buddha statue from Kamakura (11 meters high, cast from bronze) can also be seen here. Inside the lovely temple complex of Hasedera, there are various, quiet corners to be found. The photo shows a stone Jizo-statue in the middle of a group of plants. The yellow flowering *Farfugium japonicum* is a striking light point in this predominantly green garden.

HOKOKU-JI, KAMAKURA
The top part of a large, stone lantern (Ishidori) crowns this abundantly blooming *Rhododendron obtusum* hybrid. Although this garden has an un-cared for appearance, this wilderness effect is carefully managed. This garden is just as carefully cared for, as are all gardens near temples, palaces and castles that are open to visitors.

PINUS THUNBERGII
Conifers such as this beautifully trimmed pine, must always be transplanted with a large root ball. In some countries such trees are rather sloppily packed, but in Japan a complicated construction is made using straw and rope. In the background is a rough stone lantern that looks like five stones of different shapes were arbitrarily stacked on top of each other, but, in actual fact, the pieces were carefully chosen in order to achieve this natural affect.

PINUS THUNBERGII

This pine tree, with the root ball and part of the trunk protected from drying and damage, forms part of a large group of plants at a plant auction in Omiya. This 'bonsai village' of bonsai machi is only 30 minutes away from Tokyo and has been famous for centuries for bonsai culture.

In Japan it is not only the root balls which are carefully packed in this manner, but also tender, semi-hardy plants, such as palms and false sagos. They could not survive the northern regions_ season of frost and heavy snowfall without damage, without being wrapped in complicated and also, sometimes comical figures (yuki-tsuri) to wait for better, warmer times.

JISHO-JI, KYOTO

On the grounds of the Silver Pavilion is this ancient pine (*Pinus densiflora*), that with very meticulous care has grown into a giant bonsai demonstrating a well-balanced composition of branches, twigs and needles.

GARDEN MAINTENANCE, KYOTO

The maintenance of private gardens is done with as much care as temple gardens. Here, a gardener tends to a pine very meticulously. Not only are branches trimmed off; the upkeep goes so far as to remove individual, ugly pine needles. Such garden maintenance can take days and is an expensive procedure repeated a few times every year.

CASTLE OF MATSUMOTO, MATSUMOTO

One of the most beautiful castles in Japan is the one in Matsumoto. It was built in 1595 and is still completely intact. It was built of natural stone and wood. Situated inside a wide moat, this castle with its six floors was considered unconquerable. It could be well sealed against attackers and was easy to defend, but it also had, for less turbulent moments, a pavilion (tsokimi yagura) for gazing at the moon and the lovely mountainous landscape. The orange-red painted bridge that leads to the castle forms a colorful connection to the somber building which has a rather threatening appearance.

HOKOKU-JI, KAMAKURA
The former imperial city Kamakura, home to a large number of splendid temple complexes surrounded by lovely parks and gardens, lies in a mountainous region. In the photos, a dry-style garden can be seen where rocks lies like islands in a sea of raked gray gravel. In Japan such a garden is called kare-sanshui and is as much as possible a true replica of nature. The gravel is raked in circles around the islands in order to symbolize eternity. Here it is clear to see that diversity in form and optimal use of different shades of green with one color accent (tree peony) can create a garden with much beauty.

HOKOKU-JI, KAMAKURA
The photo on the last page showed the dry garden of Hokoku-ji; this picture shows the wet garden where a thin stream of water splashes out of a bamboo pipe and lands in a clear pond. The bamboo pipe is skillfully hidden in a Japanese Maple. Inspired use is made of the uneven ground in order to show the carefully pruned trees in many shades of green to their best advantage . A flowering tree peony is perfectly positioned as an eyecatcher on the edge of the gray gravel sea.

DAIHONZEN, EIHEI-JI, YOSHIDA-GUN

In a landscape that has been left as natural as possible, the little building is set off well by the large, green moss covered stones. Moss gardens are almost only to be found in Japan and that is, in part due to the moist climate. Without a lot of rain or natural springs and streams and of course painstaking care, a moss garden cannot be achieved: mosses are some of the most difficult plants to cultivate. In Japan, gardens have created with several hundreds of different sorts of mosses which produces a very colorful carpet of many shades. Such delicate moss gardens may never be walked upon, they can only be viewed from a path.

DAIHONZEN, EIHEI-JI YOSHIDA-GUN

The extensive Zen Temple complex at Eihei-ji is one of the most important and most famous Zen temples in Japan. Not only Japanese students are accepted here, but also foreigners, provided they send a written application to follow zazen (zen-meditation) well in advance. This complex draws not only many students, but it is also a top tourist attraction: bus loads of tourists are unloaded here daily! This temple complex of the Soto sect was established in 1244 and in the ensuing centuries has been continually expanded. The ancient wooden screens in the doors and windows are famous.

HOKOKU-JI, KAMAKURA
Small stone Jizo-statues in a bamboo garden at Kamakura. These extremely popular Buddhist statues are often placed by temple complexes in great numbers as protective gods for small children and especially for aborted fetuses. They are worshipped by the faithful, given flowers and food and during certain celebrations they are dressed in bib-like costumes in order to keep them warm and happy.

HOKOKU-JI, KAMAKURA
Bamboo gardens are extremely popular not only in China but also in Japan. The many large groups of different types of bamboo are a delight to the eye. This photo shows *Phyllostachys heteroclyta forma pubescens* with thick, silver gray stalks. Bamboo shoots are extremely fast growing and within a short time the young shoots can been several meters high topped with soft green leaves. The points of the young shoots that have just pushed up from the ground are especially pretty. Bamboo types that are very popular have thin black stalks and are often used in garden fencing providing an attractive background for bonsai trees. Varieties popularly planted have bright green stalks and vertical yellow stripes, whilst plants with bright yellow stalks are often used, especially against a background of dark conifers.

KATSURA IMPERIAL VILLA, KYOTO
Many types of bamboo are native to Japan and they are used in many different ways; for practical and decorative items in daily life and as plants in private and temple gardens. Bamboo stalks are often used for woven garden screen in many different ways, they are also used in clipped hedges. Behind the hedge, in the photo, the bamboo stalks have been allowed to grow to their full height for a surprising effect. They form a decorative, meters-high barrier. It hardly seems possible, but the plant race Bamboo belongs to the family of grasses (*Poaceae*). Nowadays people even use plastic bamboo garden fencing that, at first glance, cannot be distinguished from the real thing.

FUJIYA SPA HOTEL, HAKONE
Next to the Fujiya Spa Hotel, the very first hotel in Japan that was built in a western style (1878), there is a classical Japanese landscape garden, designed in the wet style. The area around Hakone has been visited for many centuries because of the hot springs, that are a strong attraction to the visiting Japanese. 'Onsen' or, hot springs are frequent vacation destinations; for the Japanese the water cannot be hot enough - it is then deliciously relaxing.

After a long visit to the springs, the visitors can, from a quiet spot, gaze at the beautifully laid out gardens; not only is the body cleansed, the spirit should also be purified. A more obvious place for this than the garden belonging to Fujiya Spa Hotel can hardly be found.

DAI-TO PAGODA, KOYASAN

This two story pagoda, lying half-hidden behind a tree turned golden yellow in color, is actually a prayer wheel. In this prayer wheel, which has a central axle that allows the pagoda to rotate, is a cylinder with Buddhist sutras (written doctrines from Buddha.) The turning of the prayer wheel actually has the same religious significance as the reciting of the sutras. In Japan there are hardly any prayer wheels to be found, in contrast to Tibet, where there are many prayer wheels, large and small, even hand-driven prayer wheels that are kept in motion by the faithful. The Donjogaran monastery, to which the Dai-to or large pagoda belongs, was established in 816 by the monk Kobo Daishi, who also established the Shingon order. After his death, Bobo Daisho was buried in the spacious temple grounds and in the ensuing centuries, the famous 'city of the dead in Koya-san.' arose around his grave.

HASEDERA TEMPLE, KAMAKURA

The park with its many smaller temple buildings is known for its beautiful garden arrangements and the interesting plants. Next to the small temple building in the photo is a group of Cycas palms (*Cycas revoluta*) a native Japanese plant that does not belong to the palm family, but belongs to the family Cycas. In the colder, northern regions of Japan, the Cycas palms are always carefully packed in straw for the winter; without protection they could not survive the cold northern winters. In late May or early June, the flowering season of the tree peony, large groups of visitors come here to enjoy the many blossoms on the great collection of plants with their white, red, pink and double flowered blossoms.

1 000 YEAR OLD GINKGO BILOBA, SENDAI

The venerable Ginkgo (Icho) of Sendai, is one of the oldest, most famous Ginkgoes in the world and is worshipped as a Shinto Kami (diety). To indicate the tree's holy character, a shimenawa (cord of rice straw) is tied around the enormous trunk. This cord also keeps angry spirits at a distance. The marvelous growths on this respectable Ginkgo in Sendai resemble stalactites and are called 'chi-chi' or mother's breasts. These chi-chi are only found on old trees and are worshipped by Shinto-followers. Prayerboards (ema) are sold to childless women. By hanging such prayerboards and calling to the Kami in prayer, childless women beg for protection from the gods or give thanks for answered prayers.

Ginkgo trees can be traced back several millions years old in plant history and are considered living fossils. These stately trees originate from China. They are often planted next to Shinto sanctuaries. They appear to be rather tough street trees which do well even when planted in busy cities with lots of air pollution

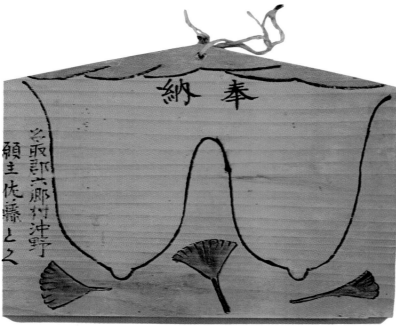

such as Tokyo and Kyoto. There are female and male specimens, the female specimens have small golden-yellow fruit in the fall that look like little plums. The flesh of the fruit smells strongly of rancid butter and is removed. The nut that is revealed, is then roasted, peeled and eaten. Gingko seeds are a popular delicacy. In temple gardens they are collected as quickly as they fall to the ground and sold for high prices in fruit and vegetable stores.

KENROKUEN GARDEN, KANAZAWA

This garden was laid out in 1676 by Tsunanori and is, along with the Kairakuen garden in Mito and the Korakuen garden in Okayama, one of the most beautiful and important Japanese gardens designed in the classic landscape style.

SHOJOSHIN-IN TEMPLE, KOYASAN

On the flattened mountain Koyasan is a large temple complex that forms the headquarters of the Shingo school, where monks are trained in esoteric Buddhism. Not only are the temples and the gardens inside this large complex are worth visiting, but also the richly wooded surroundings that invite relaxing walks. These attractions draw the many thousands of visitors that come to see the temples and gardens daily, especially in the summer season. In the early and late hours of the day, before visitors arrive, the many temple buildings and the lovely old pines trimmed as giant bonsai trees can be quietly admired and photographed. In the fall, one can marvel at the fantastic yellow and gold colored leaves from the Oriental cherry, Japanese maple, Ginkgoes and Zelkovas.

KENROKUEN GARDEN, KANAZAWA

This famous garden gets its name from the literal meaning of kenroku: a 'combination of six' special qualities. These qualities are isolation, vastness, creation by man, old age, an abundance of water, and a wide view. This landscape-style garden was designed in 1676 and has these six qualities. Since the 17th century the Kenrokuen garden has gradually grown into a large park; in the beginning of the 19th century the park was completed by the 13th master, Noriyaso. The park was opened for visitors in 1872 and has an area of slightly more than 10 hectares. About 5,000 trees have been planted, some 3,500 shrubs and there are also lovely, natural-looking paths meandering among the waterfalls and beautiful stone lanterns.

HIGASHI HONGAN-JI TEMPLE, KYOTO

Ema, or prayerboards, in written or unwritten form are bought in large numbers by the faithful. The boards are often straight, whitewood planks inscribed with a wish or prayer of thanks that can be bought at small temple stores. It is also possible to inscribe your own message: for this purpose black felt pens are always available. The boards are sometimes sawn into the shape of a simple temple, or they may also be shaped like a gourd. Sometimes they are decorated with dogs, ships or even cars. The Higashi Hongan-ji Temple was established in the end of the 16th century by Shogun Tokugawa

Ieyasu and was rebuilt in 1895 after a destructive fire. The large paper lantern is decorated with a stylized branch of the Kiri (*Paulownia tomentosa*), the emblem of the Ashikawa family that also built the Golden Pavilion (Kinkaku-ji) in Kyoto.

HASEDERA TEMPLE, KAMAKURA

The Hasedera Temple enjoys much fame because of the enormous number of Jizo statues. these small stone statues are the sacred protectors of travelers and children.

During the childrens festival, the statues are dressed in order to keep them warm and to gain their benevolence. These little god statues provide enormous support,

especially to women who have lost a child through miscarriage or abortion. They belong to the most popular and most worshipped of Buddhist gods.

SHIRAKAWA-GO OPEN AIR MUSEUM

In this rural open air museum, there are a number of beautiful old houses from the Shirakawa-go district have bee brought together and have be put on view to visitors. The houses were built in the Gassho-zukuri style for the wealthier citizens of the area. The residents lived in the ground floor, where a fireplace or irori was the central point for the family life during the long cold winters. The space in the top floor was used as storage space, but also for the raising of silk worms. The angled straw roofs are said to resemble hands folded in prayer (gassho-zuku ri); and on their slanted sides, the often thick, heavy layer of snow doesn't lie long.

MOUNT FUJI

The holy mountain Fuji is one of the highest mountains in Japan with an altitude of 3776 meters. The holy mountain Fuji-san (san is Chinese for mountain) is the result of volcanic action. The last time this volcano was active was in 1707 when ash covered the streets on Tokyo 100 kilometers away. During the months of July and August, when the snow is gone, Fuji San can be climbed; untrained climbers are prohibited from doing so during the other months of the year.

In the foreground of the photo stands Susuki or *Miscanthus sinensis*, a tall growing native Japanese plant in the grass family.

KIYOMIZUDERA TEMPLE, KYOTO

The pagoda of Kiyomizudera has three floors and towers high above the lovely shrubs and the edge of the pond with its pruned bushes. The pointed pike (Sorin) on the roof is made from nine bronze rings that symbolize the nine kingdoms of heaven. It is crowned by a bronze decoration, the Sui-en.

A CER PALMATUM
It is no wonder that the Japanese maple or *Acer palmatum* is so popular in temple and private gardens; there is no other tree that can surpass the red fall colors of the maple leaves.

GINKGO BILOBA

The yellow fan-shaped leaves of the *Ginkgo biloba* are very popular in Japan; these trees are also frequently planted in temple and private gardens. This is also an outstanding street tree and it is even possible to trim the branches very close to the trunk every year. In Japan this is done preferably in autumn, shortly before the leaves fall because it is then unnecessary to clean up fallen leaves. The favorable climate assures strong, young shoots the following year.

KONGOBU-JI, KOYASAN

Different sorts of flowering Prunus have beautiful fall colors. In particular *Prunus serrula*, that also has a lovely shiny, red brown bark, *Prunus serrulatea*, the famous Japanese Prunus with its many hybrids and *Prunus subhirtella varieteit autumnalis*, a small flowering Prunus that has a second flowering season when the fall weather is favorable, are all known for their beautiful leaf colors in the autumn. A short period of cold or frost enhances the coloring. On the other hand, if the fall is mild, there may be hardly any fall colors to be seen, to the great disappointment of the many admirers.

GINKGO BILOBA

The Ginkgo is a very ancient tree that is often planted near temples. It is a strong tree, with several variations. There are Ginkgoes with hanging branches, Ginkgoes with rising branches and even hybrid variegated leaves. In mild, cooler climates, it is a lovely tree that doesn't grow quickly, but which in time can grow really high and wide.

SHOJOSHIN-IN TEMPLE, KOYASAN

The extensive Shojoshin-in Temple complex lies in the mountainous regions tucked between ancient conifers. The trees and plants around the temple building are pruned to shape and the transition from cultivated trees to the natural woods is almost undetectable. Such gardens in the hills are called Tsukiyama in Japan.

PRUNUS SERRULATEA HYBRID
The Japanese oriental cherry with pink blossoms is a popular tree world-wide; when visiting a Japanese garden it is surprising to discover that lovely white blooming specimens also exist that really stand out when the trees carrying their radiant, pure white blossom are planted against a background of sober, dark green conifers.

KIYOMIZUDERA TEMPLE, KYOTO

The present orange-painted Kiyomizudera Temple dates to 1633, but there has been a Buddhist temple on this site since one was established in the honor of the goddess Kannon in the year 798. The main building rests on 139 columns with a length of 15 meters and has an incomparable view of Kyoto. Not so very long ago there were plans to develop a neighboring site with skyscrapers. However, the site was bought in order to prevent the plans and protect the beauty of the temple. Within the hilly temple grounds lies the Otawa waterfall; if someone drinks or bathes in the holy water they are assured of a long and healthy life on earth. The color combination of the orange building with the pink cherry blossoms is very daring to western eyes, but it is often seen at Japanese temples.

INDEX